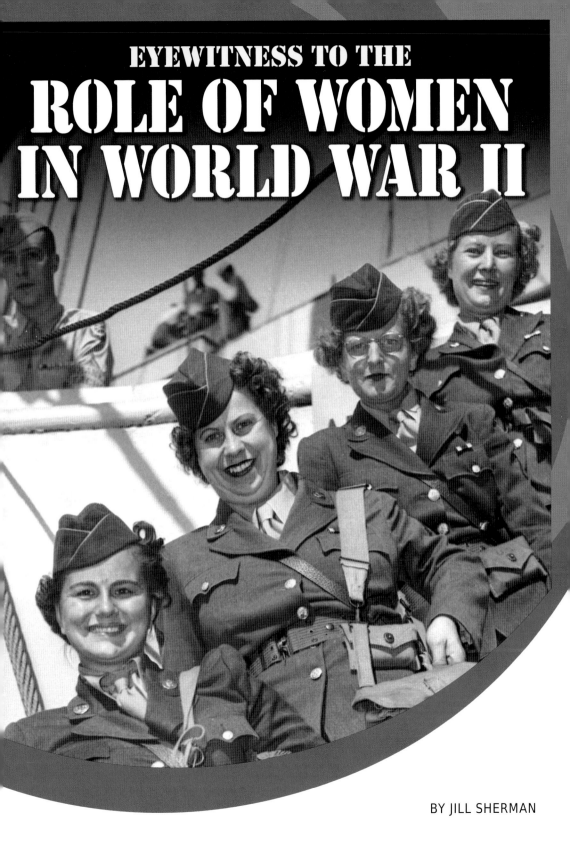

EYEWITNESS TO THE
ROLE OF WOMEN
IN WORLD WAR II

BY JILL SHERMAN

Published by The Child's World®
1980 Lookout Drive • Mankato, MN 56003-1705
800-599-READ • www.childsworld.com

Acknowledgments
The Child's World®: Mary Berendes, Publishing Director
Red Line Editorial: Design, editorial direction, and production
Photographs ©: Bettmann/Corbis, cover, 1, 10, 14, 22, 25, 29; Everett Historical/
Shutterstock Images, 4, 6; Adolph Treidler/Library of Congress, 9; AP Images, 12,
26; Ann Rosener/Farm Security Administration/Office of War Information/Library of
Congress, 17; Underwood & Underwood/Corbis, 18; Bradshaw Crandell/United States
Army/Library of Congress, 21

ISBN 9781634074193

LCCN 2015946269

Printed in the United States of America
Mankato, MN
December, 2015
PA02281

ABOUT THE AUTHOR

Jill Sherman lives and writes in Brooklyn, New York. She has written more
than a dozen books for young readers. She is thrilled to be sharing the
stories of the brave and intelligent women who helped the war effort.
Sherman is training to run a 10K race and enjoys taking photos of her dog.

TABLE OF
CONTENTS

Chapter 1

A TIME OF WAR

Cornelia Fort lived in Honolulu, Hawaii. She was the first female flight instructor in the United States. On December 7, 1941, Fort took a student for his usual flying lesson. The student would fly the plane while she observed him at the controls.

As the plane soared into the sky, Fort watched carefully for other aircraft. Hawaii was home to Pearl Harbor, a U.S. Navy base. She was used to seeing military planes during flights. Pilots stayed in assigned safety zones to avoid collisions.

Suddenly, an aircraft hurtled directly toward Fort's plane. Thinking quickly, she seized the controls. Fort piloted the plane above the oncoming aircraft. Then she noticed the red circles on the other plane's wings. It was a Japanese fighter plane. The Japanese navy was attacking Pearl Harbor.

At the time, World War II had been going on for two years. The Allied Powers included Britain, France, and the Soviet Union. They were at war with the Axis Powers: Japan, Germany, and Italy. The Japanese attack thrust the United States into the conflict. On December 8, the U.S. Congress declared war on Japan. Days later, the United States declared war on Germany and Italy.

President Franklin Roosevelt urged Americans to support the war effort. "We are now at war," he declared. "We are now in it— all the way. Every single man, woman, and child is a partner in the most tremendous undertaking of our American history."[1]

Young men lined up at military centers. They signed up to fight with the army, the navy, or the Marine Corps. But as men left for battle, women also wanted to help the war effort. Some, like Fort, had special skills or work experience. Their training would help them support American troops. Other women had never worked outside the home. However, they quickly learned new skills.

▲ **Women used rationing books to keep track of food rations.**

With so many men overseas, women took control at home. They collected fabric, scrap metal, and old tires. These materials could be used for uniforms and equipment. Women and families **rationed** their food. That way, more meals could be sent to the soldiers abroad.

Women found other ways to help, too. The troops needed weapons and supplies. Almost overnight, factories began producing military equipment. Toy companies started making compasses. Typewriter companies started making rifles. With many young men abroad, factories needed more workers. The U.S. government began advertising factory jobs to women. "Do the job he left behind," said one poster.[2]

Women of all ages eagerly entered the workforce. As *Newsweek* magazine reported, "[Women] are in the shipyards, lumber mills, steel mills, foundries. They are welders, electricians, mechanics, and even boilermakers."[3]

"Women did change. They had gotten the feeling of their own money. Making it themselves. Not asking anybody how to spend it."

—*Naomi Craig, war industry worker*[4]

In earlier years, companies did not hire women for these jobs. But as more men went to war, women were needed. They had great responsibilities. Women who were making weapons knew that they had to do their work very carefully. Mistakes could cause disaster.

By 1945, one in every four women worked outside the home. These women had a direct effect on the battlefield. Some of their work went straight into the hands of U.S. soldiers. But this was not the only way women contributed to the war effort. Many worked directly with the military.

A 1942 poster celebrated women who worked in factories and ▶ offices to help the war effort.

OLDIERS *without guns*

Chapter 2

HELPING THE MILITARY

Betty "Jean" Jennings's head was bent over her work. She carefully performed her calculations. Jennings, along with a room full of other women, was determining the **trajectories** of missiles. The army desperately needed these calculations in order to hit its targets. And it needed thousands done. Each equation took

30 hours. With so much work to be done, the army **recruited** women to do the math.

The War Department needed Jennings and other women to help run the war from home. These women were often called Government Girls. Mary Ruth Hunter took a job with the government. She collected information for missions, moving mountains of paperwork each day. Hunter saw her work as her patriotic duty. "You were needed and you served," she said. "You didn't think about individual contributions."[5]

Many women's jobs were top secret. They worked in organizing **intelligence**. These women could not talk about their work with anyone. They pored over messages from the military's spies. And they shared the messages with army leaders. The information came mainly from overseas agents. Some of these spies were also women.

In March 1944, German soldiers stood in a busy train station in France. They hoped to spot spies leaving the country. An old woman passed by, lugging a giant suitcase. They paid her no attention.

Virginia Hall had passed through undetected yet again. Hall was not an old French woman. She was a young American

▲ **Some women worked for the U.S. Navy Yard, sending and receiving messages.**

spy. She worked for the Office of Strategic Services (OSS). Hall was good at her job. She helped Allied prisoners escape. She helped the U.S. Army send supplies to its units. And she shared information about the movements of enemy troops.

Some French and German leaders knew Virginia Hall as the "Limping Lady." They gave warnings about her to their troops.

One message read, "The woman who limps is one of the most dangerous Allied agents in France. We must find and destroy her."[6]

Another OSS agent was Marlene Dietrich. She was a German-American singer and movie star. Dietrich often performed for troops. She sang her heart out to boost **morale** for American soldiers. But she also used her talent against the German army.

Before performing the song "Lili Marlene" for German soldiers, Dietrich suddenly shouted, "Boys, don't sacrifice yourselves!"[8] She urged them not to fight. German leaders were furious. They banned Dietrich's songs. The penalty for listening to them was death. But many German soldiers continued to listen to her music.

"There's a new army on the Potomac—the bright-eyed, fresh-faced young Americans who have poured into Washington from remote farms, sleepy little towns, and the confusion of cities, to work for the government in a time of national emergency. Every morning they flow, like bright rivers, into . . . the great buildings."

—Good Housekeeping, *January 1942*[7]

Chapter 3

ARMY NURSES

During wars, nurses are ready to go wherever wounded soldiers need them. World War II was no different. More than 59,000 American nurses served during the war. Many worked in **field hospitals**. Nurses also worked on hospital trains, ships, and planes.

In December 1941, Muriel Phillips was a nursing student. She was working in a doctor's office in Massachusetts. One day, she heard a speech by President Roosevelt on the office radio. The president gravely announced that the United States was at war.

Soon, army recruitment posters were plastered all over the country. They said, "Your Country Needs You."[9] Phillips was eager to support American soldiers. As soon as she could, she joined the Army Nurse Service.

Even for a nursing student, training was difficult. Phillips sweated through hours of exercises. She had to crawl through mud while **ammunition** was fired all around her. Phillips was thrilled when her training was done. But she was also nervous. She could be shipped off to any part of the world.

First, Phillips was sent to Britain to nurse injured soldiers. She brought her rations, uniform, and gas mask. Two years later, Phillips was sent to Belgium. The Germans soon started bombing the area. They wanted to destroy nearby railways. Phillips kept taking care of her patients. "The work has been hard and the hours long," she wrote. "But I really feel satisfied now because we're doing the stuff we came overseas for, and they really need us."[10]

Soldiers were fighting in Europe, Africa, and the Pacific. American nurses went to all of these places. Nurse Juanita Redmond was **stationed** in the Philippines. At first, Redmond worked in safety. Planes brought injured soldiers to the hospital, away from the battle lines. On April 6, 1942, everything changed. "Someone yelled, 'Planes overhead!'" Redmond remembered. "But those had become such familiar words that most of us paid them little attention. I went on pouring medications, and then the drone of the planes was lost in the . . . roar of a crashing bomb."[11]

Enemy planes had attacked the hospital. Bombs had torn off the roof. Nurses and doctors scrambled to save their patients. Many were trapped under rubble. As nurses worked, more wounded soldiers stumbled into the hospital. Meanwhile, Japanese forces continued to drop bombs.

"We worked wildly to get to the men who might be buried, still alive, under the mass of wreckage, tearing apart the smashed beds to reach the wounded and the dead. These men were our patients, our responsibility."

—Juanita Redmond, army nurse[12]

▲ Nurses Frances Bullock and Eleanor Whalen stood outside the Walter Reed Hospital in Washington, DC, in 1943.

That night, Redmond hid in a **foxhole**. She could not sleep. And she could not understand why enemy soldiers would bomb a defenseless hospital. It was already full of injured men. Redmond decided that "this isn't a war in which anybody—*anybody*—is let off. Each single individual . . . is in it and each must give everything he has to give."[13]

Nurses made great sacrifices to help injured troops. They knew that during a war, no one is truly safe. Enemy actions killed 16 army nurses. But nurses were not the only ones who were taking on dangerous work. Many other women served overseas. For the first time, American women served in uniform as part of the armed services.

17

Chapter 4

ARMED SERVICES

"Life in the armed services is hard and uncomfortable, but I think women can stand up under that type of living just as well as men," said First Lady Eleanor Roosevelt.[14] She was addressing the nation on her radio show, "My Day."

By 1942, the war was stretching the resources of the U.S. Army. It needed troops for combat with the enemy. It also needed people to work in non-combat jobs. Traditionally, women did not take any roles in the military. But soon, women began to serve in many military jobs. If they served as radio operators, electricians, and air traffic controllers, men who had previously held these jobs could serve in combat.

In July 1942, Elizabeth Pollock volunteered for the Women's Army Auxiliary Corps (WAAC). She was from Des Moines, Iowa. Other women came from California, Virginia, New York, Arizona, and Oregon. They were all there for the same purpose. The women wanted to serve their country. In July 1943, the organization was renamed the Women's Army Corps. Women in the corps were called WACs. As a WAC, Pollock earned military status.

Pollock's training was brutal. Each day, Pollock lined up with the other women at 6:00 a.m. She completed drills and exercises. She learned military rules. One day, Pollock and the other recruits were trained in avoiding chemical weapons. They learned to use their gas masks. The women even smelled samples of the different chemicals that might be used against them. At night, Pollock fell into bed exhausted. The next day, she would do it all again.

After four weeks of training, Pollock was ready for her assignment. She could be sent somewhere in the United States. Or she could be sent to Africa, Europe, or Asia. Wherever she went, Pollock's job would free up a man for combat.

Finally, Pollock received her assignment. She would work with the Aircraft Warning Service (AWS). Workers in AWS used instruments to identify enemy planes. Then they alerted authorities about the sightings.

Pollock was not fighting on the front lines. But women like her were not free from danger. About 140,000 WAACs and WACs served during the war years. The women worked through bombings and other attacks. They served with courage and dignity.

Not everyone supported the idea of women going overseas with the military. Some doubted women's ability to perform military work. But Pollock and other WACs proved their skills. General Douglas MacArthur was an Allied commander. He called WACs his "best soldiers."[15] In fact, during the war, women would serve in every branch of the military.

Posters encouraged women to show patriotism ▶
by becoming WACs.

Are you a girl with a Star-Spangled heart?

JOIN THE WAC NOW!

THOUSANDS OF ARMY JOBS NEED FILLING!

Women's Army Corps United States Army

Chapter 5

FLY GIRLS

In 1943, Margaret Phelan Taylor was ready for an adventure. She was 19 years old and finished with school. When *Life* magazine published a story on women pilots, Taylor was fascinated. Her brother was training to be an army pilot. She realized that she could become a pilot, too.

Unlike her brother, Taylor could not be trained by the army to fly. Women had to pay for their own pilot lessons. Taylor borrowed $500 from her father. She traveled to the Women Airforce Service Pilots (WASPs) training headquarters in Sweetwater, Texas. Taylor had to pass a physical exam to become a pilot. She was healthy. But she was a half-inch shorter than the 5-foot, 2-inch (1.5-m) minimum height. As a nurse measured her, Taylor slyly stood on tiptoe.

Dressed smartly in her WASP uniform, Taylor flew over American soil. She and the other women pilots were known as "fly girls." Mainly, they brought planes to different locations where they were needed. Taylor flew nearly every type of military aircraft, from large bombers to smaller fighter planes.

Flying these aircraft could be risky. During one of Taylor's flights, the cockpit began to smoke. She was supposed to jump out if anything went seriously wrong with the plane. But Taylor kept a cool head. She remembered thinking, "You know what? I'm not going until I see flame. When I see actual fire, why, then I'll jump."[16] The problem turned out to be a faulty instrument. The other parts of the plane were not damaged. Taylor landed safely at her destination.

Not all WASPs were as lucky. Women pilots did not fly in combat, but flying remained dangerous. A total of 38 female

> "I did it for the fun. I was a young girl and everybody had left and it was wartime. You didn't want to get stuck in a hole in Iowa; you wanted to see what was going on."
>
> —Margaret Phelan Taylor, WASP[17]

pilots were killed while flying for their country. Military leaders honored their service. However, the women did not receive military funerals.

General Henry Arnold commanded the U.S. Army Air Forces. At first, he doubted women pilots' skills. He was not sure "whether a slip of a girl could fight the controls of a B-17 in heavy weather." But by 1944, he had changed his mind. That year, Arnold spoke at a graduation ceremony for new WASPs. He admitted that "it is on the record that women can fly as well as men."[18]

Two WASPs paused for a photograph after graduating from ▶ their training program at Ellington Field near Houston, Texas.

Chapter 6

THE HIGH SEAS

While WASPs flew the skies, WAVES, SPARs, and Marine Corps Women's Reserve members sailed the seas. These women worked with the navy, Coast Guard, and Marine Corps.

Mary Lyne and Kay Arthur worked for the Coast Guard. They served as SPARs, a name from the Coast Guard motto *Semper Paratus: Always Ready.* Many SPARs used radio signals to calculate locations of ships.

◄ Private Marion Chadwick, part of a group of women Marines, learned to operate a large weapon in 1943.

Lyne and Arthur proudly wore their uniforms. But some people were startled or angry to see women in military clothing.

Once, a man stopped Lyne and Arthur on the street. He asked why they were serving. He seemed surprised that the women would volunteer for the Coast Guard. But later that day, the women boarded a bus. The driver wouldn't accept their nickels for the fare. He thanked them for their work.

Uniformed women first had jobs answering phones and filing paperwork. But many determined women soon earned more challenging jobs. WAVES (Women Accepted for Voluntary Emergency Service) served as naval air navigators. Some took jobs as airplane machinists. Others worked to decode enemy communications.

Slowly, many people's attitudes about military women changed. "We were a new idea to America," wrote Lyne and Arthur.[19] Eventually, most Americans came to accept women in uniform.

After several hard years, World War II ended in 1945. Japan, Germany, and Italy all surrendered to the Allies. Women returned home from their assignments abroad. Almost 400,000 women had served in uniform. Some women in uniform were killed or wounded in the line of duty.

At home, many women also left their wartime jobs. Men returned to their old factory and office careers. But women had proven that they could do this work. In the years after the war, more women began to work outside the home.

Women had helped win World War II for the Allies. They had also changed Americans' ideas about what women could do. As Mary Lyne and Kay Arthur wrote, "When the great histories of this war are written, historians will not overlook the part we played."[20]

A group of WAVES and WACs visited the Navy Yard in ▶ Philadelphia, Pennsylvania, to learn about ship repairs.

GLOSSARY

ammunition (am-yuh-NISH-uhn): Material fired from a weapon is ammunition. During the war, factories produced weapons and ammunition.

field hospitals (FEELD HOS-pi-tulz): Field hospitals are temporary hospitals set up to support military troops. Some army nurses worked in field hospitals to care for injured soldiers.

foxhole (FOKS-hole): A foxhole is a small pit that soldiers use to take shelter during a battle. When the hospital was attacked, an army nurse took cover in a foxhole.

intelligence (in-TEL-i-juns): Intelligence is secret information about an enemy. Spies gathered intelligence and shared it with the U.S. military.

morale (muh-RAL): Morale is remaining cheerful and positive even during hard times. Entertainers tried to keep up morale among U.S. soldiers.

rationed (RASH-und): When something is rationed, the supply is limited and people are allowed to have only a specific amount. Food was rationed during World War II.

recruited (ri-KROOT-ed): When people are recruited, they are invited to join an organization. Women were recruited for many jobs during World War II.

stationed (STEY-shund): When people are stationed somewhere, they are assigned to a post in a specific location. Military workers were stationed in different parts of Europe and the Pacific.

trajectories (truh-JEK-tuh-reez): Trajectories are the paths of flying objects. Women calculated trajectories of different weapons so the soldiers could hit their targets.

SOURCE NOTES

1. "The US Home Front at a Glance." *The National WWII Museum.* National WWII Museum, n.d. Web. 31 July 2015.

2. "Do the Job He Left Behind." *Hagley Digital Archives.* Hagley Museum and Library, n.d. Web. 31 July 2015.

3. Sybil E. Hatch. *Changing Our World: True Stories of Women Engineers.* Reston, Virginia: ASCE, 2006. Print. 178.

4. Sharon H. Hartman Strom and Linda P. Wood. "Women and World War II." *What Did You Do in the War, Grandma?* Brown University Scholarly Technology Group, 1997. Web. 31 July 2015.

5. "Partners in Winning the War: American Women in World War II." *National Women's History Museum.* National Women's History Museum, 2007. Web. 31 July 2015.

6. Kathryn J. Atwood. *Women Heroes of World War II.* Chicago: Chicago Review Press, 2001. Print. 198.

7. Megan Rosenfeld. "'Government Girls': World War II's Army of the Potomac." *Washington Post.* The Washington Post Company, 10 May 1999. Web. 31 July 2015.

8. Kathryn J. Atwood. 217.

9. "Cadet Nurse Corps Posters from World War II." *Reminisce.* RDA Enthusiast Brands, 2015. Web. 31 July 2015.

10. Kathryn J. Atwood. 209.

11. Judy Barrett Litoff and David C. Smith, eds. *American Women in a World at War.* Wilmington, DE: Scholarly Resources, 1997. Print. 85.

12. Ibid. 86.

13. Ibid. 89.

14. Eleanor Roosevelt. "My Day: Women in War." *American Experience.* PBS, 2013. Web. 31 July 2015.

15. Melissa K. Wiford. "'My Best Soldiers': Thirty-Six Years of the Women's Army Corps." *Army.mil.* United States Army Military History Institute, 2008. Web. 31 July 2015.

16-18. Susan Stamberg. "Female World War II Pilots: The Original Fly Girls." *Morning Edition.* NPR, 9 March 2010. Web. 31 July 2015.

19-20. Judy Barrett Litoff and David C. Smith, eds. 57.

TO LEARN MORE

Books

Adams, Simon. *World War II*. New York: DK Publishing, 2014.

Bearce, Stephanie. *Spies, Secret Missions, and Hidden Facts from World War II*. Waco, TX: Prufrock, 2015.

Kramer, Ann. *Women and War: World War II*. New York: Franklin Watts, 2015.

Web Sites

Visit our Web site for links about the role of women in World War II: childsworld.com/links

Note to Parents, Teachers, and Librarians: We routinely verify our Web links to make sure they are safe and active sites. So encourage your readers to check them out!

INDEX